INSIDE THE NFL

St. Louis Rams

BY
ZACH WYNER

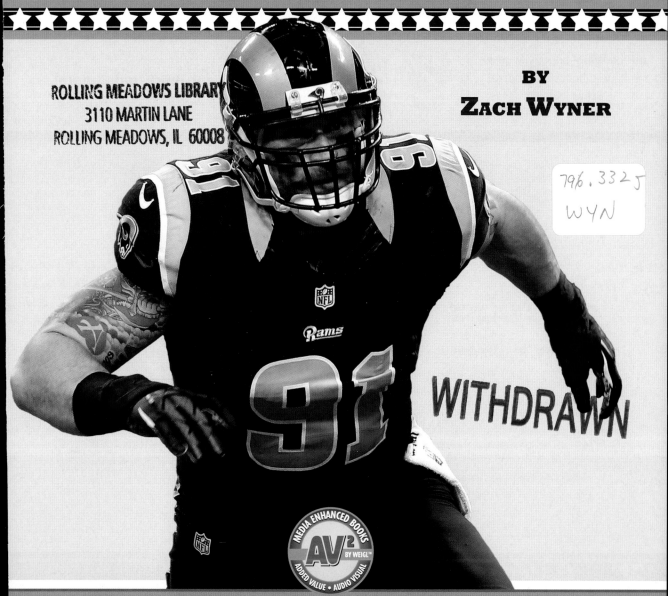

MEDIA ENHANCED BOOKS
AV2 BY WEIGL
ADDED VALUE · AUDIO VISUAL

www.av2books.com

AV² provides enriched content that supplements and complements this book. Weigl's AV² books strive to create inspired learning and engage young minds in a total learning experience.

Your AV² Media Enhanced books come alive with...

Audio
Listen to sections of the book read aloud.

Key Words
Study vocabulary, and complete a matching word activity.

Go to www.av2books.com, and enter this book's unique code.

Video
Watch informative video clips.

Quizzes
Test your knowledge.

BOOK CODE

L 9 3 2 9 6 9

Embedded Weblinks
Gain additional information for research.

Slide Show
View images and captions, and prepare a presentation.

AV² by Weigl brings you media enhanced books that support active learning.

Try This!
Complete activities and hands-on experiments.

... and much, much more!

Published by AV² by Weigl
350 5th Avenue, 59th Floor
New York, NY 10118
Websites: www.av2books.com   www.weigl.com

Library of Congress Control Number: 2014931154

ISBN 978-1-4896-0894-9 (hardcover)
ISBN 978-1-4896-0896-3 (single-user eBook)
ISBN 978-1-4896-0897-0 (multi-user eBook)

Library of Congress Control Number: 2014931154

042014
WEP150314

Project Coordinator Aaron Carr
Art Director Terry Paulhus

Photo Credits
Every reasonable effort has been made to trace ownership and to obtain permission to reprint copyright material. The publishers would be pleased to have any errors or omissions brought to their attention so that they may be corrected in subsequent printings.

Weigl acknowledges Getty Images as its primary image supplier for this title.

St. Louis Rams

CONTENTS

Introduction

The St. Louis Rams are among the most well traveled teams in the National Football League (NFL). From the Midwest, to the West Coast, and then back again, they have been on the move since 1936, seeking out the country's most passionate football fans and leaving everything on the field.

The Rams' most memorable squads have been defined both by stars and groups of players who came to be known not by the names on the back of their jerseys, but by nicknames that defined their style of play. Individual players such as Jack Youngblood and Eric Dickerson stand apart as Ram legends who put their teams on their shoulders and led them to greatness.

The Rams are the only NFL team to win a championship in three different cities (Cleveland, Los Angeles, and St. Louis).

Nicknames such as the "Fearsome Foursome" and the "Greatest Show on **Turf**" also define periods of tremendous success. Rams teams have been champions when the talents of great athletes complimented one another, making the whole greater than the sum of its parts.

Chris Long has been a defensive end for the Rams since 2008.

ST. LOUIS Rams

Stadium Edward Jones Dome

Division National Football Conference (NFC) West

Head coach Jeff Fisher

Location St. Louis, Missouri

NFL Championships 1945, 1951, 1999

Nicknames Fearsome Foursome, Greatest Show on Turf

27
Playoff Appearances

3
NFL Championships

15
Division Championships

History

CALIFORNIA DREAMING

The Rams actually left Los Angeles in 1980, yet kept Los Angeles as part of their team name, despite playing in Anaheim, California for 15 seasons.

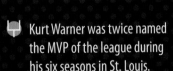 Kurt Warner was twice named the MVP of the league during his six seasons in St. Louis.

Originally from Cleveland, Ohio, the Rams spent one year as members of the All American Football League (AAFL) before joining the NFL in 1937. Behind the play of **most valuable player (MVP)** Bob Waterfield, the Cleveland Rams won the 1945 NFL Championship. In 1946, the Rams moved to Los Angeles to avoid competing with new AAFL team, the Cleveland Browns. Between 1949 and 1955, Waterfield and Norm Van Brocklin led the Rams to four NFL Championship Games. In 1951, the Rams won their second title behind a league-leading offense that featured Pro Football **Hall of Fame** receivers Tom Fears and Elroy "Crazylegs" Hirsch.

The Rams enjoyed their longest stretch of success between 1967 and 1980. Teams led by the "Fearsome Foursome" **defensive line**, and later by hall of famer Jack Youngblood, won nine division titles in 14 years. In 1979, the aging Rams won the **National Football Conference (NFC)** Championship. The 1980s were highlighted by record-setting running back Eric Dickerson and a passing attack that featured quarterback Jim Everett and receivers Flipper Anderson and Henry Ellard. After 49 years in Southern California, the Rams moved to St. Louis in 1995. Coach Dick Vermeil's "Greatest Show on Turf" took flight in 1999. Kurt Warner, Marshall Faulk, Torry Holt, Isaac Bruce, and Orlando Pace were among the stars who helped St. Louis score a then record 526 points and led the Rams to a 23-16 win over the Tennessee Titans in **Super Bowl** XXXIV.

In 1945, Bob Waterfield won a championship as the Rams' quarterback, but he could not duplicate that success as the Rams' coach. He finished with a 9-24 coaching record.

St. Louis Rams

The Stadium

Edward Jones Dome holds 66,000 fans.

The city of St. Louis broke ground on the Edward Jones Dome in 1992. While it was built to house both sports and conventions, the Dome was constructed with the desire that it would lure an NFL team to St. Louis. The city had not hosted an NFL franchise since the St. Louis Cardinals left for Arizona in 1988. Their strategy worked.

Despite the team's numerous relocations, Rams fans have remained loyal and loud.

The Rams agreed to play their home games in the Edward Jones Dome because the city of St. Louis guaranteed that the venue would be a top tier stadium through 2015. This meant that renovations would be a big part of the stadium's life cycle. Sports stadiums are constantly changing, offering fans new and better features each season. St. Louis is committed to having one of the NFL's best stadiums.

Since 1995, the Dome has witnessed the "Greatest Show on Turf" and hosted two NFC Championship Games (1999, 2001), both of which the Rams won. In addition to football-related events, the Dome has also hosted international soccer matches, the National Collegiate Athletic Association (NCAA) Final Four, and some of the world's biggest musical acts.

Hungry Rams fans can eat a slow-roasted turkey sandwich or braised beef brisket served with chips.

Where They Play

CANADA

Washington **30**

Oregon

Montana

North Dakota

Minnesota

Lake Superior

Wisconsin **23**

22

Idaho

South Dakota

Iowa

24

Wyoming

Nebraska

14

Illinois

13

29

Nevada

Utah

Colorado

Kansas

Missouri

31

15

California

16

Arizona

New Mexico

Oklahoma

Arkansas

32

Pacific Ocean

UNITED STATES

17

Texas

Mississippi

Louisiana

12

27

Alaska

Hawai'i

MEXICO

Gulf of Mexico

0   500 Miles
0   500 km

0   100 Miles
0   100 km

AMERICAN FOOTBALL CONFERENCE

EAST	NORTH	SOUTH	WEST
1 Gillette Stadium	5 FirstEnergy Stadium	9 EverBank Field	13 Arrowhead Stadium
2 MetLife Stadium	6 Heinz Field	10 LP Field	14 Sports Authority Field at Mile High
3 Ralph Wilson Stadium	7 M&T Bank Stadium	11 Lucas Oil Stadium	15 O.co Coliseum
4 Sun Life Stadium	8 Paul Brown Stadium	12 NRG Stadium	16 Qualcomm Stadium

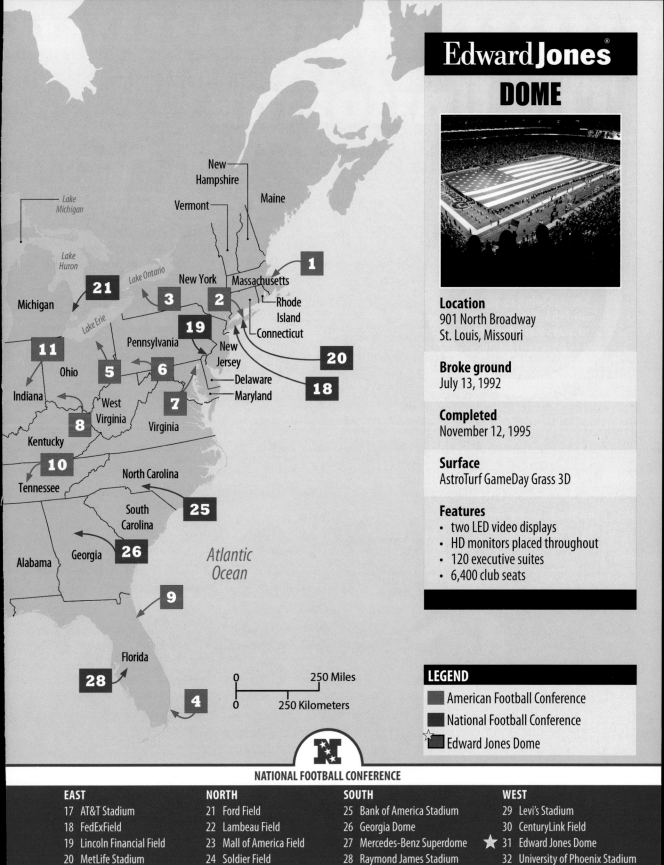

Edward Jones® DOME

Location
901 North Broadway
St. Louis, Missouri

Broke ground
July 13, 1992

Completed
November 12, 1995

Surface
AstroTurf GameDay Grass 3D

Features
- two LED video displays
- HD monitors placed throughout
- 120 executive suites
- 6,400 club seats

LEGEND
- American Football Conference
- National Football Conference
- ☆ Edward Jones Dome

NATIONAL FOOTBALL CONFERENCE

EAST		NORTH		SOUTH		WEST	
17	AT&T Stadium	21	Ford Field	25	Bank of America Stadium	29	Levi's Stadium
18	FedExField	22	Lambeau Field	26	Georgia Dome	30	CenturyLink Field
19	Lincoln Financial Field	23	Mall of America Field	27	Mercedes-Benz Superdome	★ 31	Edward Jones Dome
20	MetLife Stadium	24	Soldier Field	28	Raymond James Stadium	32	University of Phoenix Stadium

The Uniforms

TRUE BLUE

Since moving to St. Louis in 1995, the Rams have always worn their blue jerseys at home.

 Robert Quinn was named the 2013 Defensive Player of the Year by the Pro Football Writers Association.

The Rams' uniforms have changed quite a bit over the years. While alterations have been frequent, gold and blue have been the primary colors since 1937.

Currently the uniforms are navy blue with gold numbers and stripes on the jerseys and gold stripes on the pants. Away uniforms consist of white jerseys with navy blue and gold sleeves and navy blue numbers. The pants are white with navy blue and gold stripes.

The current **alternate uniform** is a throwback to the uniforms worn in Los Angeles in the 1980s and revived in St. Louis in 1995. They consist of a blue jersey with yellow-gold stripes and numbers and yellow-gold pants with a blue stripe.

The Rams have changed their uniforms four times since they moved to Los Angeles in 1946.

The Helmets

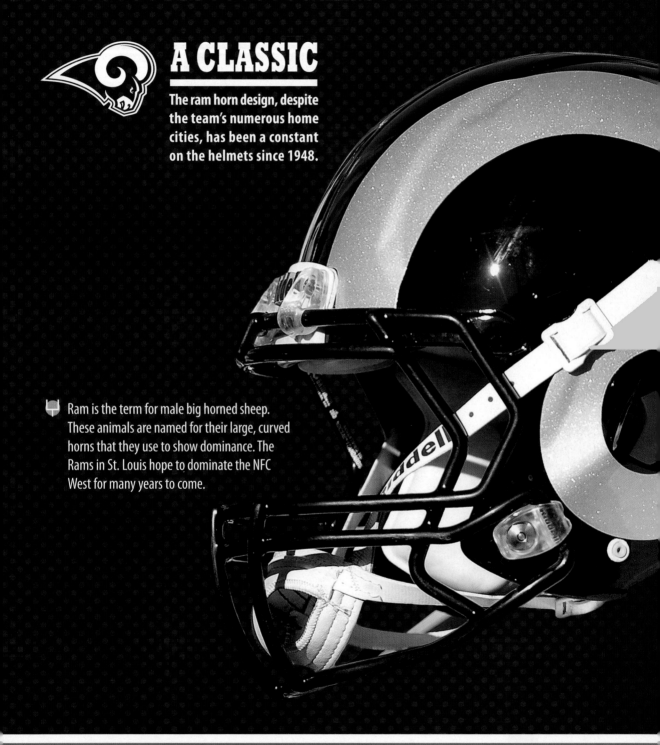

A CLASSIC

The ram horn design, despite the team's numerous home cities, has been a constant on the helmets since 1948.

Ram is the term for male big horned sheep. These animals are named for their large, curved horns that they use to show dominance. The Rams in St. Louis hope to dominate the NFC West for many years to come.

In 1948, halfback Fred Gehrke, who studied art in college and worked as a commercial artist during the offseason, painted horns on the Rams' leather helmet. The 1948 Rams became the first team whose **logo** appeared on their helmet, creating a tradition that forever changed the look of professional football.

When the NFL changed to plastic helmets in 1949, the horns no longer needed to be painted by hand. Instead, a painted design was baked into the helmets at the factory. The horns were wider, closer together at the front of the helmet, and they curved around the earhole.

These days, the logo is a decal that is applied to the helmet instead of painted on. The home and away helmets are navy blue with "old gold" horns while the alternate helmet design is blue with yellow-gold horns. All helmets feature a navy blue facemask.

 In 2004, the NFL banned single bar facemasks, saying they were unfit to protect players.

The Coaches

7 Jeff Fisher's St. Louis Rams have won seven games in each of his first two season as the head coach.

Jeff Fisher coached the Houston Oilers, who later became the Tennessee Titans, for 17 seasons, and compiled an impressive 142–120 win-loss regular season record.

The Rams have had 26 different head coaches. While most did not stay long, some of them enjoyed great success. In fact, Rams coaches such as Adam Walsh, Joe Stydahar, and George Allen departed quickly despite winning division titles and Coach of the Year awards. In Jeff Fisher, the Rams believe they have found a leader who will create the kind of stability they've rarely seen.

CHUCK KNOX

A two-time head coach of the Los Angeles Rams, Chuck Knox enjoyed incredible success his first time around, leading the Rams to five division titles in five years. Known to many as "Ground Chuck" for his team's emphasis on the running attack, Knox's teams dominated the NFC West.

DICK VERMEIL

Dick Vermeil became the Rams' head coach in 1997. In 1999, Vermeil's offense exploded for a then-NFL record 526 points. They were called the "Greatest Show on Turf" and they brought the Rams franchise its first Super Bowl victory.

JEFF FISHER

Jeff Fisher served as the head coach of the Tennessee Titans for 17 seasons before coming to St. Louis. During that time, he took the Titans from last place to American Football Conference (AFC) Champions. His teams have been called "aggressive," "edgy," "chippy," and even "dirty," but none of that has ever bothered Fisher. His primary focus is winning.

The Mascot

In 2010, the Rams became the last NFL franchise to add a mascot. Now, only four teams take the field without the support of a mascot.

With "the coating of a stuffed animal, but the build of a superhero," the Rams' new mascot Rampage has been a smash hit since his creation in 2010. Standing 6 feet, 1 inch, weighing 200 pounds, and wearing a Rams jersey with the number one on it, Rampage certainly looks capable of playing a little safety should someone get injured.

Rampage's goal is to be the first mascot on the cover of the "Madden NFL" video game.

Rampage has worked hard to try and establish a reputation as a super fan with a huge heart. During his first season in St. Louis, Rampage showed his commitment to his community, appearing at more than 300 charitable events. Rampage was rewarded for all his hard work when he was voted to the 2011 NFL **Pro Bowl**.

Rampage is the Rams' second mascot. The first was a short-lived furry creature named Ramster.

Legends of the Past

Many great players have suited up in the Rams' blue and gold. A few of them have become icons of the team and the city it represents.

Merlin Olsen

Position Defensive End
Seasons 15 (1962–1976)
Born September 5, 1940, in Logan, Utah

While Merlin Olsen may never have won an NFL Championship, his presence on the Rams' defensive line throughout the 1960s and well into the 1970s was key in making them a championship-level team. Olsen was the foundation upon which the Rams built their "Fearsome Foursome," the defensive line that terrorized opponents throughout the 1960s. Olsen's outstanding play continued right up until he retired. In his 15-year career, Olsen missed only two games. He was a first-team **All-Pro** five times, and he made the Pro Bowl an NFL-record 14 straight seasons.

Isaac Bruce

In the Rams' first season in St. Louis, Isaac Bruce established himself as the team's superstar. He was the kind of receiver who could get open even when everyone on the field knew the ball was going to him. That year, he set franchise records in receptions (119) and receiving yards (1,781). His 13 touchdowns were second only to Elroy "Crazylegs" Hirsch's 17 in 1951. In Bruce's 14 seasons with the Rams, he had more than 1,000 receiving yards eight times, made four Pro Bowls, and his 73-yard fourth-quarter touchdown reception in Super Bowl XXXIV proved to be the game winner.

Position Wide Receiver
Seasons 16 (1994–2009)
Born November 10, 1972, in Fort Lauderdale, Florida

Marshall Faulk

The "Greatest Show on Turf" owed much of its success to the brilliance of Marshall Faulk. Faulk combined explosive speed with incredible hands. As a receiver out of the **backfield**, Faulk was deadly. In 1999, he combined 1,381 rushing yards with 1,048 receiving yards to set a then-NFL record of 2,429 **yards from scrimmage**. For three straight years, from 1999 to 2001, Faulk's 5.4 yards per carry led the NFL. In 2000, his 2,189 yards from scrimmage and 31 combined rushing and receiving touchdowns earned him the NFL's MVP award. He was inducted into the NFL Hall of Fame in 2011.

Position Running Back
Seasons 12 (1994–2005)
Born February 26, 1973, in New Orleans, Louisiana

Kurt Warner

Kurt Warner is the greatest undrafted player in NFL history and one of the greatest stories in sports. After being cut by the Green Bay Packers in 1994, Warner was stocking groceries in Cedar Falls, Iowa. In 1995, he signed with the Iowa Barnstormers of the Arena Football League (AFL). When Warner finally got his shot with the Rams, he made it count. In his first season as starting quarterback, Warner led the league in completion percentage (65.1), touchdown passes (41), and **passer rating** (109.2). He became just the seventh NFL player to win both league and Super Bowl MVP in the same season.

Position Quarterback
Seasons 12 (1998–2009)
Born June 22, 1971, in Burlington, Iowa

Stars of Today

Today's Rams team is made up of many young, talented players who have proven that they are among the best players in the league.

Robert Quinn

As a rookie out of the University of North Carolina, Robert Quinn was regarded as a top **prospect** and a surefire first round pick. Happily for the Rams, he slipped to the 14th spot, where they were able to grab him with their first pick. Robert Quinn has grown as a player in each of his first three seasons with St. Louis. In 2013, his play rose to a level never before seen in a Rams' uniform. Quinn registered seven forced fumbles, 57 tackles, and set a franchise record with 19 **sacks**.

Position Defensive End
Seasons 3 (2011–2013)
Born May 18, 1990, in Ladson, South Carolina

Chris Long

Son of hall of fame lineman Howie Long, Chris Long began his NFL career with some big shoes to fill. In six seasons with the Rams, he has shown that he aims to be every bit the player his father was.

In 2011, Long registered 13.5 sacks and was voted the 2011 NFL Alumni Defensive Lineman of the Year. In 2012, he led the Rams in sacks (11.5), quarterback hits (24), and hurries (50). His 50 quarterback hurries topped NFL defensive linemen for the third-straight year.

Position Defensive End
Seasons 6 (2008–2013)
Born March 28, 1985, in Santa Monica, California

Sam Bradford

The Rams' 2010 No. 1 overall **NFL Draft** pick wasted no time in showcasing the skills that had brought him so much success at the University of Oklahoma. In his first NFL season, Sam Bradford set rookie records for most passes in a row without an interception (169) and most completions for a rookie (354). He started all 16 games, and helped the Rams improve from a disastrous 1-15 season to a respectable 7-9. While Bradford has been slowed by injury in 2011 and 2013, he continues to improve. In seven games in 2013, he had a career-best 90.9 passer rating.

Position Quarterback
Seasons 4 (2010–2013)
Born November 8, 1987, in Oklahoma City, Oklahoma

Alec Ogletree

After seeing significant playing time at the University of Georgia as a safety, Alec Ogletree was moved to the linebacker position. In his sophomore and junior seasons, Ogletree showed the terrific instincts, strength, and speed that led to the Rams making him a first-round draft pick in 2013. In his rookie season with the Rams, Ogletree led the team with 95 unassisted tackles, forced six fumbles, registered 1.5 sacks, and returned an interception 98 yards for a touchdown against the Houston Texans.

Position Linebacker
Seasons 1 (2013)
Born September 25, 1991, in Newnan, Georgia

All-Time Records

2,105
Single-season Rushing Yards

In 1984, Eric Dickerson set a single-season rushing record that stands to this day. He averaged an astounding 5.6 yards per carry.

10,135
Career Rushing Yards

For nine years, Steven Jackson was a model of consistency, rushing for more than 1,000 yards in eight straight seasons and making three Pro Bowls.

4,830

Single-season Passing Yards

In 2001, Kurt Warner completed an NFL-best 68.7 percent of his passes, led the league in passing yards, and added 36 touchdowns.

23,758

Career Passing Yards

Jim Everett threw for more than 3,000 passing yards in five straight seasons as a Ram, including a career-best 4,310 in 1989.

14,109

Career Receiving Yards

Isaac Bruce was lighting up defenses for five years before Kurt Warner came to town. For the next few seasons, Bruce was a key part of the "Greatest Show on Turf."

Timeline

Throughout the team's history, the St. Louis Rams have had many memorable events that have become defining moments for the team and its fans.

1936
The AAFL is founded and the Cleveland Rams are **charter members**. At the end of the season, owner Homer Marshman pays a $10,000 entrance fee to join the NFL.

January 20, 1980
In the Rams' first Super Bowl, Jack Youngblood plays on a broken leg. Quarterback Vince Ferragamo throws for 212 yards and the Rams lead the Pittsburgh Steelers 19-17 at the start of the fourth quarter. Sadly, two Steelers touchdowns end the Rams' extraordinary run. Shortly thereafter, the Rams move to Anaheim, California.

In 1967, the Rams go 11-1 and win their first division title since 1955.

| 1930 | 1940 | 1950 | 1960 | 1970 | 1980 |

December 16, 1945
After eight forgettable seasons, NFL MVP and Rookie of the Year Pro Bob Waterfield leads the Rams to a 9-1 record and a spot in the Championship Game against Washington. The Rams emerge with a 15-14 victory and their first NFL Championship.

1984
In Jack Youngblood's final season as a Ram, it is second-year running back Eric Dickerson that grabs the headlines, rushing for an NFL-record 2,105 yards. The Rams finish second in their division and lose a close playoff game to the New York Giants, 16-13.

1973
In their first year under head coach Chuck Knox, the Rams go 12-2 and win their division. Jack Youngblood, the man teammate Merlin Olsen calls "the perfect defensive end," makes his first of seven straight Pro Bowls, and Lawrence McCutcheon gains 1,386 yards from scrimmage.

January 30, 2000
In Super Bowl XXXIV, MVP Kurt Warner throws for 414 yards and two touchdowns. Isaac Bruce and Torry Holt each have more than 100 receiving yards, and Rams linebacker Mike Jones tackles Tennessee receiver Kevin Dyson at the one-yard line as time expires to preserve a 23-16 victory.

After 49 years in Southern California, the Rams move to St. Louis in 1995.

The Future
A brief glimpse at the 2013 Rams' schedule reveals a team that was better than their record. Despite Sam Bradford only playing in seven games and despite some tough early-season losses, the Rams rebounded for big wins against Indianapolis, Chicago, and New Orleans. With Bradford torching defenses, and Long and Quinn terrorizing opposing quarterbacks, look for Jeff Fisher's St. Louis Rams to be a factor in the highly competitive NFC West.

| 1990 | 1995 | 2000 | 2005 | 2010 | 2015 |

1999
In his third year as head coach, Dick Vermeil's offense takes off under former AFL star Kurt Warner. Warner throws 41 touchdown passes, Marshall Faulk gains 2,429 yards from scrimmage, and the "Greatest Show on Turf" bests Tampa Bay's NFL-best defense to win the NFC Championship.

In Super Bowl XXXVI, despite a fourth quarter comeback by the Rams, they are upset, 20-17, by the New England Patriots.

2004
Marshall Faulk and rookie Steven Jackson lead a strong ground attack while Marc Bulger throws for nearly 4,00 yards. In the wild card round, the Rams beat NFC West division rivals Seattle, 27-20, in the franchise's last playoff win to date.

Write a Biography

Life Story

A person's life story can be the subject of a book. This kind of book is called a biography. Biographies often describe the lives of people who have achieved great success. These people may be alive today, or they may have lived many years ago. Reading a biography can help you learn more about a great person.

Get the Facts

Use this book, and research in the library and on the Internet, to find out more about your favorite Ram. Learn as much about this player as you can. What position does he play? What are his statistics in important categories? Has he set any records? Also, be sure to write down key events in the person's life. What was his childhood like? What has he accomplished off the field? Is there anything else that makes this person special or unusual?

Use the Concept Web

A concept web is a useful research tool. Read the questions in the concept web on the following page. Answer the questions in your notebook. Your answers will help you write a biography.

Concept Web

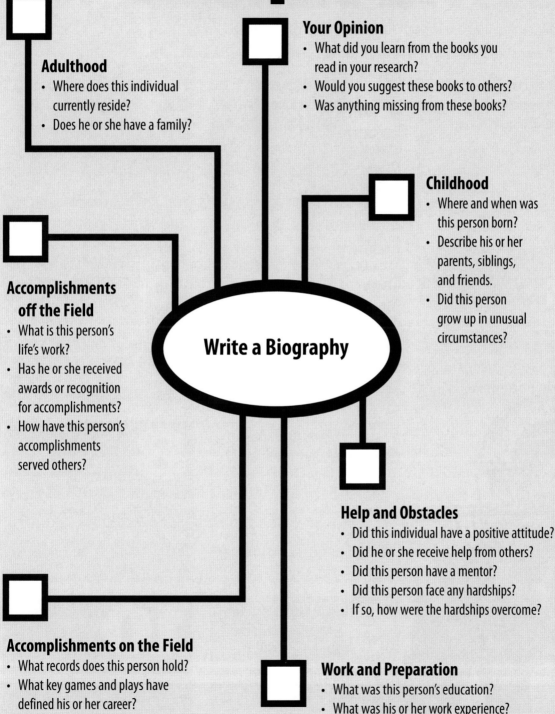

Adulthood
- Where does this individual currently reside?
- Does he or she have a family?

Your Opinion
- What did you learn from the books you read in your research?
- Would you suggest these books to others?
- Was anything missing from these books?

Childhood
- Where and when was this person born?
- Describe his or her parents, siblings, and friends.
- Did this person grow up in unusual circumstances?

Accomplishments off the Field
- What is this person's life's work?
- Has he or she received awards or recognition for accomplishments?
- How have this person's accomplishments served others?

Write a Biography

Help and Obstacles
- Did this individual have a positive attitude?
- Did he or she receive help from others?
- Did this person have a mentor?
- Did this person face any hardships?
- If so, how were the hardships overcome?

Accomplishments on the Field
- What records does this person hold?
- What key games and plays have defined his or her career?
- What are his or her stats in categories important to his or her position?

Work and Preparation
- What was this person's education?
- What was his or her work experience?
- How does this person work; what is the process he or she uses?

Trivia Time

Take this quiz to test your knowledge of the St. Louis Rams.
The answers are printed upside-down under each question.

1 How many Super Bowls have the Rams won in their history?

A. One

2 In what three cities have the Rams won NFL Championships?

A. Cleveland, Los Angeles, St. Louis

3 Which Ram played on a broken leg in the 1980 Super Bowl?

A. Jack Youngblood

4 Which Rams running back owns the NFL single-season rushing record?

A. Eric Dickerson

5 Which Rams running back set a then-NFL record for yards from scrimmage in 1999?

A. Marshall Faulk

6 How many sacks did Robert Quinn record in 2013 to set a new Rams' record?

A. 19

7 When did the Rams win their first NFL Championship?

A. December 16, 1945

8 Which Rams hall of fame receiver was nicknamed "Crazylegs"?

A. Elroy Hirsch

9 What was the nickname of the Rams' defensive line in the 1960s?

A. The Fearsome Foursome

10 How many straight Pro Bowls did Rams hall of fame lineman Merlin Olsen play in?

A. 14

Key Words

All-Pro: an NFL player judged to be the best in his position for a given season

alternate uniform: a uniform that sports teams may wear in games instead of their home or away uniforms

backfield: the area of play behind either the offensive or defensive line

charter members: original or founding members of an organization

defensive line: defensive linemen line up directly on the line of scrimmage, close to the ball. There are two positions usually considered part of the defensive line: defensive tackle (DT) and defensive end (DE)

hall of fame: a group of persons judged to be outstanding in a particular sport

logo: a symbol that stands for a team or organization

most valuable player (MVP): the player judged to be most valuable to his team's success

National Football Conference (NFC): one of two major conferences in the NFL along with the American Football Conference (AFC)

NFL Draft: an annual event where the NFL chooses college football players to be new team members

passer rating: a rating given to quarterbacks that tries to measure how well they perform on the field

Pro Bowl: the annual all-star game for NFL players, pitting the best players in the National Football Conference against the best players in the American Football Conference

prospect: a player who is likely to succeed in a sport at a high level

sacks: a sack occurs when the quarterback is tackled behind the line of scrimmage before he can throw a forward pass

Super Bowl: the NFL's annual championship game between the winning team from the NFC and the winning team from the AFC

Turf: grass and the surface layer of earth held together by its roots

yards from scrimmage: the total of rushing yards and receiving yards from the yard-line on the field from which the play starts

Index

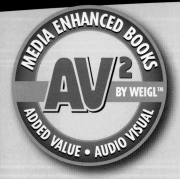

Log on to www.av2books.com

AV² by Weigl brings you media enhanced books that support active learning. Go to www.av2books.com, and enter the special code found on page 2 of this book. You will gain access to enriched and enhanced content that supplements and complements this book. Content includes video, audio, weblinks, quizzes, a slide show, and activities.

AV² Online Navigation

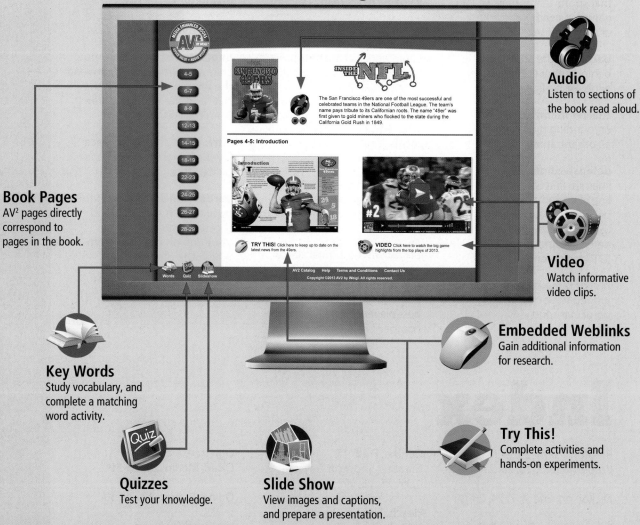

Book Pages
AV² pages directly correspond to pages in the book.

Audio
Listen to sections of the book read aloud.

Video
Watch informative video clips.

Embedded Weblinks
Gain additional information for research.

Key Words
Study vocabulary, and complete a matching word activity.

Try This!
Complete activities and hands-on experiments.

Quizzes
Test your knowledge.

Slide Show
View images and captions, and prepare a presentation.

AV² was built to bridge the gap between print and digital. We encourage you to tell us what you like and what you want to see in the future.

Sign up to be an AV² Ambassador at www.av2books.com/ambassador.

Due to the dynamic nature of the Internet, some of the URLs and activities provided as part of AV² by Weigl may have changed or ceased to exist. AV² by Weigl accepts no responsibility for any such changes. All media enhanced books are regularly monitored to update addresses and sites in a timely manner. Contact AV² by Weigl at 1-866-649-3445 or av2books@weigl.com with any questions, comments, or feedback.